CAT BREEDS

PERSIAN CATS

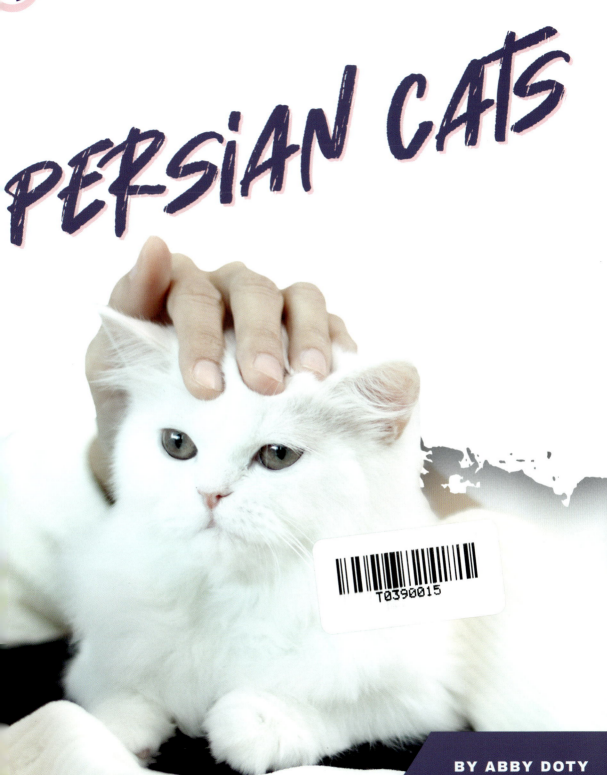

BY ABBY DOTY

WWW.APEXEDITIONS.COM

Copyright © 2025 by Apex Editions, Mendota Heights, MN 55120. All rights reserved. No part of this book may be reproduced or utilized in any form or by any means without written permission from the publisher.

Apex is distributed by North Star Editions:
sales@northstareditions.com | 888-417-0195

Produced for Apex by Red Line Editorial.

Photographs ©: Shutterstock Images, cover, 1, 4–5, 6, 7, 8–9, 10–11, 12, 13, 16–17, 18, 19, 20, 21, 22–23, 24–25, 26, 27; Library of Congress, 14–15, 29

Library of Congress Control Number: 2024944885

ISBN
979-8-89250-312-9 (hardcover)
979-8-89250-350-1 (paperback)
979-8-89250-425-6 (ebook pdf)
979-8-89250-388-4 (hosted ebook)

Printed in the United States of America
Mankato, MN
012025

NOTE TO PARENTS AND EDUCATORS

Apex books are designed to build literacy skills in striving readers. Exciting, high-interest content attracts and holds readers' attention. The text is carefully leveled to allow students to achieve success quickly. Additional features, such as bolded glossary words for difficult terms, help build comprehension.

TABLE OF CONTENTS

CHAPTER 1
CUDDLY CATS 4

CHAPTER 2
BREED HISTORY 10

CHAPTER 3
FURRY FELINES 16

CHAPTER 4
CAT CARE 22

COMPREHENSION QUESTIONS • 28
GLOSSARY • 30
TO LEARN MORE • 31
ABOUT THE AUTHOR • 31
INDEX • 32

CHAPTER 1

CUDDLY CATS

A girl is visiting her grandparents. She sits near a window and pets their Persian cat. The Persian watches squirrels running outside.

Persian cats often rest in sunny spots.

Persians need to be brushed or combed every day.

The girl grabs a comb. She runs it through the cat's fur. Soon, all the tangles are gone. The Persian lets out a soft **purr**.

FAST FACT
Most Persians don't meow much. But the cats may purr when happy.

A Persian's thick coat tangles easily. Combing keeps the fur smooth and soft.

Most Persian cats love being petted and cuddled.

That night, the girl gets into bed. The cat curls up next to her. They fall asleep together.

CALM CATS

Persian cats are gentle and calm. They do not need a lot of exercise. And they don't make very much noise. So, they can be good pets for **elderly** people.

CHAPTER 2

BREED HISTORY

The Persian cat's exact origins are not known. The **breed** probably came from long-haired cats that lived in Persia. By the 1600s, people had brought these cats to Europe.

Persia is now called Iran. This country is in the Middle East.

Persians likely got some of their looks from Turkish Angora cats.

In Europe, people mixed the cats from Persia with other long-haired breeds. Over time, the cats **developed** thicker fur. They got new colors, too.

ROYAL CATS

Queen Victoria ruled Britain from 1837 to 1901. She owned many Persian cats throughout her life. Because of her, Persians became **popular** among British royals.

Several Persian cats lived in Buckingham Palace with Queen Victoria.

Persian cats continued spreading to different parts of the world. They were made an official breed in 1906. Today, many people own Persians.

In the late 1800s, owners started bringing Persians to cat shows.

FAST FACT

Early Persians had long noses. In the 1950s, people bred them to have flatter faces.

CHAPTER 3

FURRY FELINES

Persians cats are medium sized. They can weigh up to 12 pounds (5 kg). The cats are known for their short **muzzles**. They have wide, flat faces.

Many Persians' faces look like they have been pressed flat.

Persians also have long fur. It comes in many different colors and patterns. The fur is very soft. But it tends to shed a lot.

A Persian's fur has two layers. The topcoat is long and soft. The undercoat is short.

Some owners cut their Persians' hair short. This style is called a lion trim.

FAST FACT
A Persian's thick fur can cause the cat to overheat.

Most Persians are social. The cats enjoy being close to people.

Persians have **stocky** bodies and short legs. So, the cats are not good jumpers or climbers. Instead, they are easygoing. Most are friendly with people and animals.

LAP CATS

Persians tend to be less active than other breeds. And loud noises can make the cats feel stressed. So, Persians prefer living in calm homes. They enjoy lounging around and sitting on people's laps.

Persians spend lots of time sleeping.

CHAPTER 4

CAT CARE

Besides daily combing or brushing, Persian cats need baths every week. Regular grooming can help prevent **matted** fur. It also limits shedding.

Matted fur can hurt cats. Brushing gets rid of painful knots.

Persians have watery eyes. Tears may drip down the cats' flat muzzles and **stain** their fur. Owners should clean their Persians' faces every day.

FAST FACT

Flat faces can cause breathing problems for Persians.

Owners can use small, damp cloths to wash their cats' faces.

Persians can gain weight easily. So, they need to exercise every day. Owners should play with their cats to help them stay active. Owners should also make sure not to feed them too much.

Persians enjoy playing short, easy games with their owners.

Flat-faced cats are at risk for tooth and gum problems. So, owners should brush their cats' teeth often.

EATING AND DRINKING

Persians often have trouble eating and drinking. Their flat faces may not be able to reach food or water in deep bowls. Flat dishes and water fountains can help.

COMPREHENSION QUESTIONS

Write your answers on a separate piece of paper.

1. Write a few sentences explaining the main ideas of Chapter 4.

2. Would you like to own a Persian cat? Why or why not?

3. When were Persians made an official breed?
    - A. 1837
    - B. 1901
    - C. 1906

4. What would happen if a Persian was not brushed?
    - A. Its fur would get fewer stains.
    - B. Its fur would get more matted.
    - C. Its fur would stop shedding.

5. What does **origins** mean in this book?

The Persian cat's exact origins are not known. The breed probably came from long-haired cats that lived in Persia.

    A. what something cost
    B. how something looks
    C. how something started

6. What does **grooming** mean in this book?

Besides daily combing or brushing, Persian cats need baths every week. Regular grooming can help prevent matted fur.

    A. petting an animal's fur
    B. caring for an animal's fur
    C. dirtying an animal's fur

Answer key on page 32.

GLOSSARY

breed
A specific type of cat that has its own look and abilities.

developed
Changed over time.

elderly
Old or aging.

matted
Having thick, tangled clumps.

muzzles
The jaws and noses of animals.

popular
Liked by or known to many people.

purr
A low, vibrating sound.

stain
To leave a mark on something.

stocky
Wide and sturdy.

BOOKS

Jaycox, Jaclyn. *Read All About Cats*. North Mankato, MN: Capstone Publishing, 2021.

Pearson, Marie. *Cat Behavior*. Minneapolis: Abdo Publishing, 2024.

Watts, Robyn. *Clever Cats!* Sandgate, Queensland, Australia: Knowledge Books, 2024.

ONLINE RESOURCES

Visit **www.apexeditions.com** to find links and resources related to this title.

ABOUT THE AUTHOR

Abby Doty is a writer, editor, and booklover from Minnesota.

B
breathing, 24
breeds, 10, 12, 14, 21
Britain, 13

C
calm, 9, 21

E
Europe, 10, 12
exercising, 9, 26

F
faces, 15, 16, 24, 27
fur, 6, 12, 18–19, 22, 24

G
grooming, 22

M
muzzles, 16, 24

O
origins, 10
overheat, 19
owners, 24, 26

P
Persia, 10, 12

V
Victoria (queen), 13

ANSWER KEY:
1. Answers will vary; 2. Answers will vary; 3. C; 4. B; 5. C; 6. B